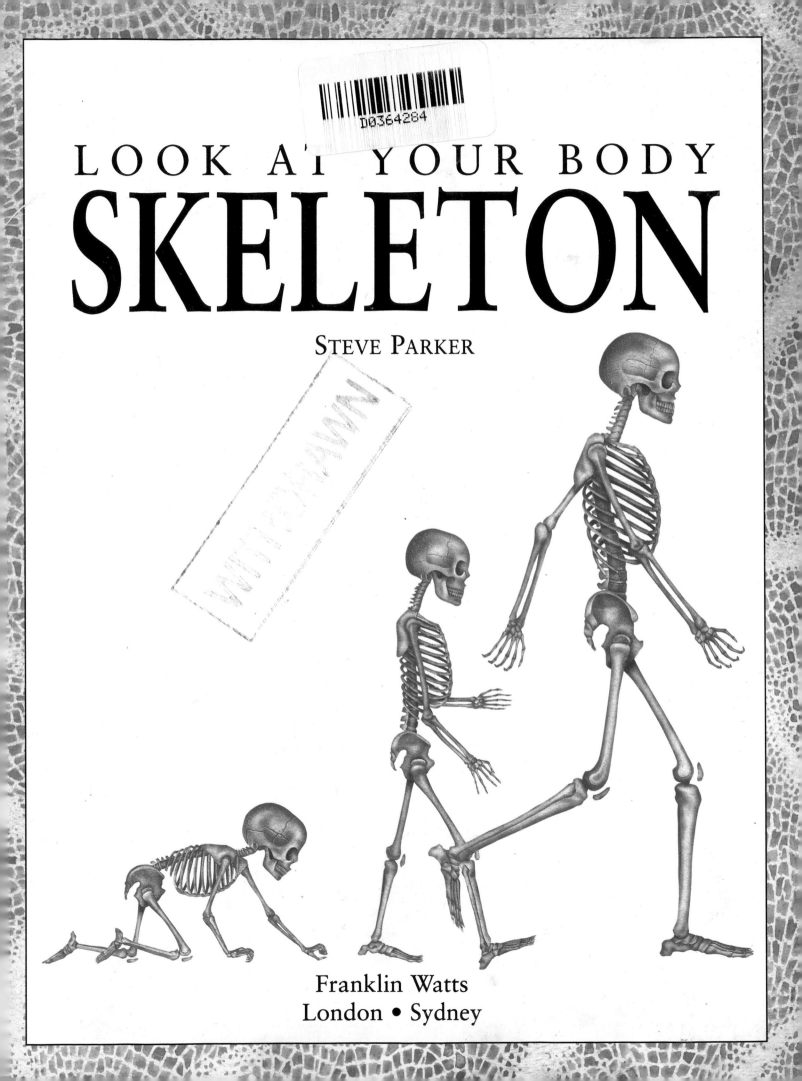

LOOK AT YOUR BODY
SKELETON

STEVE PARKER

Franklin Watts
London • Sydney

An Aladdin Book
© Aladdin Books Ltd
1996
All rights reserved
Designed and
produced by
Aladdin Books Ltd
28 Percy Street
London W1P 0LD

*First published in
Great Britain in 1996
by Franklin Watts*
96 Leonard Street
London EC2A 4RH

ISBN 0 7496 2461 2

*A catalogue record
for this book is
available from the
British Library.*

Printed in Belgium

Editor Jon Richards

Design

David West •
CHILDREN'S BOOK DESIGN
Designer Ed Simkins
Illustrator
Ian Thompson
Picture research
Brooks Krikler
Research
Consultant
Dr R Levene MB.BS,
DCH, DRCOG

Steve Parker has
written over 100
books for
children, many
of those concerning
human anatomy and
physiology.

CONTENTS

4 SHAPE UP!

6 UNDER YOUR SKIN

8 THE BONE'S STRUCTURE

10 THE SKULL

12 THE SPINE & PELVIS

14 THE RIBCAGE

16 THE SHOULDER, ARM & HAND

18 THE HIP, LEG & FOOT

20 CARTILAGE

22 BETWEEN THE BONES

24 THE GROWING SKELETON

26 THE AGEING SKELETON

28 HEALING BONES

30 KNOW YOUR BODY!

31 GLOSSARY

32 INDEX

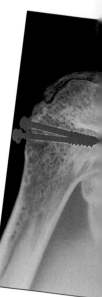

INTRODUCTION

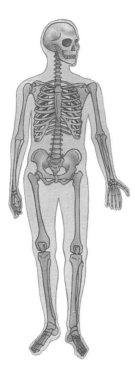

LOOK AT YOUR BODY! Even though you and your friends may vary greatly in size, you'll see that all of you have a very definite shape, with a certain number of limbs, a head and a body. What keeps you in this shape and stops you from sliding into a sloppy mess?

The answer lies with the strong framework found inside you (above left). Called the skeleton, it is made up from hundreds of bones (below right). This bony structure lies under the skin, hidden from view for most of the time. Until recently it was only normally possible to see the bones of dead people or the remains of bones from creatures that have been dead for millions of years (top right).

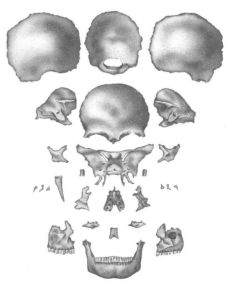

Today, doctors are able to look at your skeleton without having to cut you open. By using X-rays and scans, they can see through your skin, muscles and other soft tissues to examine your bones and check whether they have been damaged (left).

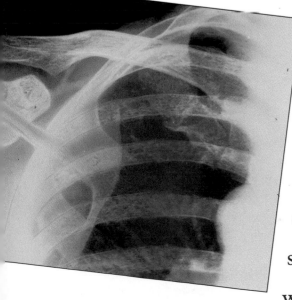

SHAPE UP!

DESPITE THE GREAT variety of animal shapes in nature, all creatures need to have some way of keeping their bodies from collapsing or falling apart.

Some, called vertebrates, have an internal skeleton, made out of bone or cartilage. The skeleton is centred around a backbone. It supports the body's shape and protects the internal parts. Vertebrates include mammals, such as humans and horses, fish, such as sharks, and birds.

Others have no internal skeleton and need different ways of keeping their body shape, such as a hard outer skeleton. These animals are collectively known as invertebrates, and they include crustaceans, such as lobsters, molluscs, such as slugs, and jellyfish.

JELLYFISH
This beautiful creature has no solid skeleton to support its body. Instead, its shape is maintained by water-filled, soft inner tissues, over which its outer layers are stretched. Take a jellyfish out of water, and its body will collapse.

SLUG
As with the jellyfish, a slug keeps its body shape by stretching its skin over fluid-filled body parts. The slug, however, is not supported by water, like the jellyfish. The pressure from inside keeps its body from collapsing.

LOBSTER
The lobster is surrounded by a rigid skeleton, like a suit of armour. Although it protects the lobster, it prevents growth and is shed each time the animal grows. It is also very heavy, and makes the lobster clumsy when placed out of water.

HORSE
Like you, the horse has an internal skeleton of bone to support its body. Instead of walking on two legs, its skeleton is one of a powerful, four-legged runner, with long leg bones and large neck bones to support a heavy head.

4

SHARK

Sharks, such as the whale shark (left), and other related fish, including rays and dogfish, have skeletons that are made from gristle (cartilage). This substance is like bone, but more flexible. These creatures are called cartilaginous fish.

BONY FISH

Other fish have skeletons made from bone (see X-ray, above). Known as bony fish, they all have a central spinal column on which the ribs, skull and fins are anchored. The fish's muscles can pull on this framework, enabling the fish to arch its body and tail to one side and then to the other, in order to swim through the water.

HUMAN

Your skeleton is made mostly from a material called bone. Its shape is unique to humans, having developed over millions of years to produce an animal that can walk upright on two legs. The large skull holds a big brain with which to think. The hands can grasp objects firmly or pick up, hold and manipulate the most delicate items.

SUPPLE, STRONG AND MOBILE

The bones in your skeleton fulfil a number of different roles. They protect your soft internal parts as you move about and play a sport (left). The skeleton also allows your body to move, by giving the muscles levers to pull against. Bones also contain marrow which makes the tiny blood cells that flow through your veins and arteries. Finally, your skeleton acts as an important store for minerals that are needed by the body. These minerals are found in crystals that, along with fibres of collagen (see page 9), make up bone tissue.

UNDER YOUR SKIN

BENEATH YOUR FRAGILE skin sits the incredibly complex structure that forms your skeleton. By the time you become an adult this skeleton will have 206 different bones, which give your body its shape and protect its internal organs. The bones are divided into two groups – the axial skeleton of the head and torso, and the appendicular skeleton of the limbs. Bones can also be grouped by their shapes, which reflect their different roles, such as long bones, short bones and flat bones.

IRREGULAR BONES
These do not fit neatly into any of the other categories of bones. They include the hip bones, some of the bones of the face and the vertebrae (right). The vertebrae vary in shape (see page 12) depending on where they are in your backbone.

FLAT BONES
Instead of being flat, these bones are in fact curved or thin, like plates. Their large surface area helps muscles to attach to them. Or, in the case of the skull bones, such as the parietal bone (right), they protect the internal organs. Flat bones include the sternum (breast bone) and the scapulae (shoulder blades).

LONG BONES

These bones are longer than they are wide. They are found in your arms and legs, such as the fibula (above) which is found in your lower leg. With the help of muscles, these bones act as levers to help you walk about and lift things.

SESAMOID BONES

Named after sesame seeds, which they are thought to look like, these bones lie inside tendons, the cord-like tissues that connect muscles to bones. They are usually found sitting over a joint, such as the patella (kneecap, right). These bones help to protect the tendon and aid in joint movement.

SHORT BONES

Short bones are usually as wide as they are long, and shaped like blocks. They occur in parts of the body where movement is fairly restricted. They include the carpal bones of the wrists and the tarsal bones of the feet (left).

Axial skeleton

Appendicular skeleton

AXIAL AND APPENDICULAR SKELETONS

The central part of the body, on which the other parts anchor themselves, is called the axial skeleton. It includes the skull bones, the spine, the ribs and the sternum. The rest is called the appendicular skeleton. It is made up from the appendages or extremities. These include arms, hands, fingers, hips, shoulders, arms, hands, fingers, legs, feet and toes.

7

If a person has a problem with the production of blood cells by the bone marrow, as with the disease leukemia, he or she may require a bone-marrow transplant (right). Testing for a suitable donor is very rigorous because the donated marrow must match the patient's very closely to prevent the body rejecting it. Marrow from the donor is then removed by syringe and given to the sufferer. The new marrow will hopefully produce normal blood cells to replace those damaged by the disease.

COMPACT BONE

SPONGY BONE

MARROW
The cavity in the middle of a typical long bone is filled with a substance known as marrow (below). At the heads (epiphyses) of some bones, such as the femur, the cavity is filled with red bone marrow. This important substance makes most of the blood cells that flow through your body.

BLOOD VESSELS
A rich network of blood vessels runs throughout the skeleton. The blood brings nutrients and minerals to the bones, allowing bones to maintain themselves. It also takes away waste products.

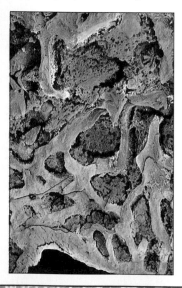

PARTS OF THE BONE
A typical long bone (above and right) can be split into five parts. The head of the bone at either end is known as the epiphysis. Below this is the neck, called the metaphysis. Finally, the main body or shaft of the bone is known as the diaphysis.

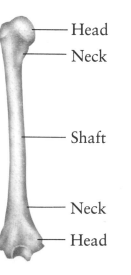

— Head
— Neck

— Shaft

— Neck
— Head

THIN MEMBRANE
The outside of the bone is covered by a thin membrane, called the periosteum. This is made from fibres and can be turned into bone tissue when the bone is growing, or if it is fractured.

The BONE's STRUCTURE

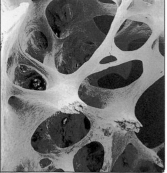

SPONGY BONE
Also known as cancellous bone, this forms a lattice-like pattern throughout the interior of the bone (above). This lattice makes the bone very light and very strong, allowing it to cope with the stresses and strains of moving about. In between the lattice's fingers of bone, known as trabeculae, sits the bone marrow.

IN MOST BONES, bone tissue is arranged in two different structures; compact bone and spongy bone. These are most apparent in long bones (see main illustration), such as the femur. Rather than static, bones are continuously maintaining and repairing themselves to suit the needs of the body

The bone tissue itself is a mixture of bendy fibres of collagen and rigid mineral crystals. Together, these make the skeleton very strong and flexible. The skeleton also contains less water than the rest of the body. On average, the human body is made up of 62 percent water. In bone tissue, water makes up 20 percent.

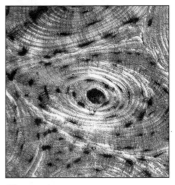

COMPACT BONE
This forms the outer layer of bone. Under a microscope you can see that it is formed from hundreds of cylinders, called Haversian systems (above). These are made up of layers (lamellae), that surround a tube (Haversian canal), through which the blood vessels and nerves run. Embedded within the concentric bone layers are tiny bone cells called osteocytes (below).

9

Lamellae

Haversian canal

Blood vessels

Nerve

Close-up of Haversian system

Bone cell

The SKULL

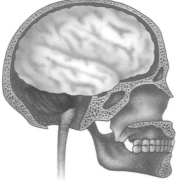

THE BONES THAT make up the skull are some of the most important bones in the entire skeleton. They form a protective case around the delicate brain and eyes. They also provide a firm framework for various muscles, such as those used to move the eyes, to bite and chew when eating and to make facial expressions like smiling. The smaller bones at the front of the skull also form a person's distinctive facial features.

BRAIN CASE
The whole skull contains 28 bones (below). The rigid case that holds the brain, called the cranium (above), is formed by eight bones. The front 14 bones are the facial bones. These range from the very small bones in the nose, to the large bones of the jaw. All of these bones are fixed firmly together at joints, called sutures. There are also six tiny bones found in the ear.

10

SKULL BONES
1 Parietal
2 Occipital
3 Temporal
4 Frontal
5 Zygomatic
6 Sphenoid
7 Lacrimal
8 Ossicles
9 Palatine
10 Vomer
11 Ethmoid
12 Inferior nasal concha
13 Nasal
14 Maxilla
15 Mandible

SINUSES
These are four cavities in the skull that act as resonating chambers for the voice and make the skull lighter. You may have noticed how your voice changes when you have a cold and your sinuses become blocked.

Sinuses

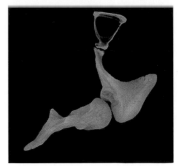

EAR BONES
The two sets of three tiny bones inside the ears are called the auditory ossicles, and they are the smallest bones of the whole skeleton. Each set is comprised of the malleus (hammer), incus (anvil) and the smallest, the stapes (stirrup), which is only about 5 mm ($\frac{1}{4}$ inch) long. Despite their small size, they have joints, nerves, blood vessels and some muscles attached, just like larger bones.

HEARING
Sound waves pass into the ear, causing the eardrum to vibrate. The ear bones (ossicles) then transfer these vibrations into the cochlea, which converts the vibrations into nerve signals.

FRONTAL BONE

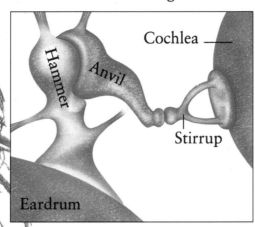

Cochlea

Hammer

Anvil

Stirrup

Eardrum

11

MAXILLA BONE

JAW MOVEMENTS
Try moving your jaw in different directions – up and down, side to side, even forwards and backwards (right). The jaw joint is just in front of the ear. Its flexible range of movements allows you to chew food and to speak clearly. The maxillae or upper jaw is immovable, being firmly fixed to the rest of the skull.

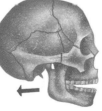

MANDIBLE

Hyoid

HYOID
This bone sits under the base of your tongue, just above your "Adam's apple". The hyoid is firmly held in place by a large number of ligaments and muscles.

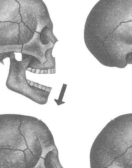

Vocal cords

Windpipe

SPEAKING
As air is forced up the windpipe (left), muscles stretch the vocal cords, which the passing air vibrates. This creates your voice. These muscles are fixed to the hyoid, without which you could not speak.

The SPINE & PELVIS

THE SPINE, also called the spinal column or backbone, forms the central support for the skeleton and houses the spinal cord. It is made of linked bones known as vertebrae. Some animals like snakes can have more than 100 vertebrae (below left). A human, like you, has 33 vertebrae, some of which have become fused to form 26 actual bones. These are divided into cervical vertebrae in the neck, thoracic vertebrae in the chest and lumbar vertebrae in the lower back. Below the lumbar vertebrae is the sacrum, and finally the coccyx – all that is left of your "tail". Attached to the sacrum is your pelvis. This bowl-shaped structure holds the leg joints and supports many of your internal organs, such as your intestines and bladder.

7 Cervical

12 Thoracic

5 Lumbar

Sacrum

Coccyx

Spinal cord

SPINAL CORD
Each vertebra has a wide part or body to the front, and a vertebral arch to the rear. The arches line up to form a tunnel. This contains the spinal cord, the body's main bundle of nerves which extends down from the brain. The spine acts as a bony tube that protects the cord (right).

Vertebra

Disc

VERTEBRAL JOINTS
Between the vertebrae are pads of cartilage, called intervertebral discs. These allow each vertebra to tilt slightly against its neighbours. Over the whole spine, these small movements make the spinal column very flexible. With practice, a person can make his or her spine very supple (above).

The problem known as a "slipped" disc affects an intervertebral disc. The disc presses on the small nerve roots which join to the spinal cord just behind it, causing a sharp pain in the back. This pain may shoot down the arm or leg. However, it is very rare for the whole disc to slip out of position and press on the nerves. Instead, a soft portion of the intervertebral disc is squeezed out like toothpaste from a tube, and presses on the nerves. This is more correctly called a prolapsed disc.

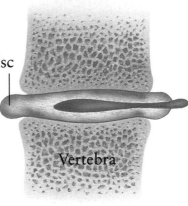

Disc

Vertebra

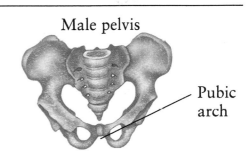

Male pelvis

Pubic arch

THE MALE PELVIS

The pelvis is formed by the sacrum and coccyx at the rear, and the paired ilium, ischium and pubis at the front. The male pelvis is heart shaped (above), with a slim pelvic opening and a narrow pubic arch.

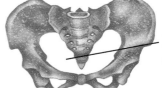

Female pelvis

Pelvic opening

THE FEMALE PELVIS

In contrast to the male pelvis, the female pelvis, being broader and flatter, is generally kidney shaped (above). It has a wide pelvic opening and a wide pubic arch. Together, these help a baby to slip through the pelvis at birth.

ILIUM

SACRUM

Pubis

Coccyx

Ischium

The RIBCAGE

STAND BY A mirror and look at your chest. You'll see the cage-like structure of your ribs lying just beneath the skin.

Unlike the hard, protective outer casing, or exoskeleton, of an insect such as a beetle (above), the human ribcage is not rigid. It is flexible, to help with the muscle-powered movements of breathing. At the same time it protects the lungs, heart and other internal organs. The 12 pairs of ribs are long, curved bones that join to the thoracic vertebrae at the rear. At the front ends, the ribs are made of cartilage, known as costal cartilage.

The upper seven pairs, known as the "true ribs" join via their costal cartilage to the wide, flat sternum, or breastbone. The eighth to tenth pairs of ribs join to the sternum indirectly, via the costal cartilage of the seventh pair of ribs. Because of this they are known as "false ribs".

PROTECTIVE SHIELD
As with the breastplate on a suit of armour (above), the ribcage protects the soft organs beneath. However, it remains flexible enough to withstand impacts and allow breathing movements.

COSTAL CARTILAGE
This forms an extension to the true bone at the front and rear part of each rib. Together with the bone, the cartilage forms a springy cage that will bend rather than break when an object hits the chest.

FLOATING RIBS
The eleventh and twelfth pairs of ribs do not extend around to the front of the chest. Instead, their front ends are embedded in the muscle layers of the chest wall.

14

THE CHEST

The ribcage protects the upper body, or chest, from knocks and pressure. The floor of the chest is formed by an upward-domed muscle called the diaphragm. This means that some parts which lie below the diaphragm, such as the stomach on the left of your body and the liver on the right, stick up inside the protective shield of the ribcage (right).

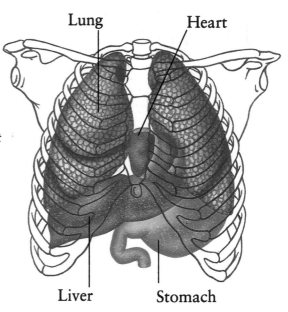

Lung   Heart

Liver   Stomach

STERNUM

The breastbone, or sternum, is a dagger-shaped bone at the front of the chest. It is split into three main parts and is joined directly to the costal cartilage of the upper seven pairs of ribs and with the clavicles (collar bones).

RIBS AND SPINE

Each rib has three movable joints (left). One is at the front, where it joins to the sternum through a link of costal cartilage. At the rear, the rib is joined with the vertebra in two places. At the end of the rib, it joins with the main part of the vertebra. The other rear joint is against the transverse process, which sticks out from the vertebra.

Rib

Vertebra

Transverse process

Sternum

S T E R N U M

BREATHING

When breathing in, the dome-shaped diaphragm, which lies below the lungs, contracts and flattens. At the same time the muscles which lie between the ribs contract, pulling the ribs up and out, making the ribcage bigger (top). These movements expand the lung size and draw in air. To breathe out, the diaphragm returns to its dome shape and the rib muscles relax. The lungs spring back to their smaller size, pushing out air.

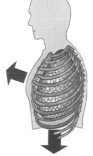

Breathing in

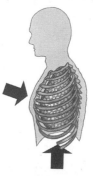

Breathing out

15

The SHOULDER, ARM & HAND

YOUR TWO UPPER limbs, the arms, are the most mobile parts of your body. You can move them in a huge circle from front to back, and take them from the side of your leg to behind your head. Not only that, they bend in the middle at the elbow, and near the end at the wrist. This makes them very flexible to use. Add a gripping tool to the end, that can powerfully grasp a rope or delicately manipulate a pen, and you can see how important the shoulder, arm and hand are to you.

SCAPULA

HUMERUS

ANIMAL "HANDS"
Mammals have a varied collection of forelimbs. The wings of the bat (below) are made from a thin membrane and enable it to fly, whereas the flippers of a sea lion are thickly webbed to help it swim. However, if you look at the skeletons of these animals, you will see that mammals, including humans, have the same bones. They all have a scapula (shoulder blade), a humerus, radius, ulna (arm bones) and finger bones.

Bat

——— Fingers

Sea lion

Humerus ———

Radius ———

Ulna

——— Fingers

Scapula

POWERFUL ARMS
Just as the leg bones are able to support the body, so can the arm bones (right). However, the arm muscles are not as strong as in the legs and, without training, you would soon get tired if you remained in a handstand for long.

RADIUS AND ULNA
These two long bones make up your forearm. Together, they act as a lever to lift the hand. They also allow the forearm to twist in a half-circle, letting you see either your palm or the back of your hand.

RADIUS

ULNA

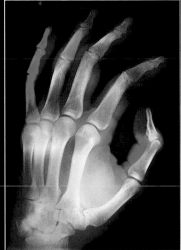

POWER GRIP
This is the strongest grip that the hand can use. Here, the fingers are wrapped around an object, while the thumb grips from the other side. This is employed when holding a hammer (right) or climbing a rope.

HOOK GRIP
As well as being strong, this grip is relatively inflexible. Here, the fingers are looped, forming a hook, for example to pick up a case (above).

INTRICATE WORK
Humans are not the only animals to have opposable thumbs (thumbs that can grip things) – monkeys and apes have them, too. However, no other animal can use them as delicately as you. This allows you to hold the tiniest object between the thumb and any finger, letting people do intricate work such as watch-making (above).

HAND AND WRIST
Each wrist is made up of eight small bones, known as carpals. The palm of the hand is formed from five metacarpal bones. Fourteen small phalanges make up the four fingers and the thumb (left).

PRECISION GRIP
The most delicate way to hold something, this allows an object to be manipulated between the thumb and the tips of the fingers. Such a grip allows the hand to become an extremely useful tool. For example, it can be used to hold the bow of a violin or a pencil (below).

Thumb

Index finger

Middle finger

Ring finger

Little finger

Palm bones

Carpals

Carpals   Metacarpals   Phalanges

The HIP, LEG & FOOT

THE LOWER HALF of your body's skeleton, from the top of your hips to the tip of your toes, is made from 62 bones. Together this collection of bones has to support your body weight as you stand, and must also act together to help you walk or run from place to place. All of this can be achieved with an incredible level of agility and speed. Top international sprinters can run at 36 km/h (22 mph).

At the top is the femur, which sits firmly in the pelvis, allowing the leg to swing back and forth. Below this lie the knee joint and the two bones of the lower leg, the tibia and fibula. At the base, supporting the whole body, is the foot.

HIP JOINT

— Pelvis

The head of the femur or the socket may become damaged, either by old age or injury. If so, then part of, or the whole hip joint may have to be replaced (left). In a conventional total-hip-replacement operation, the head of the femur is removed. A metal ball, fixed to the bone by a metal shaft, is put in its place. The damaged socket is then replaced with a plastic cup. However, this plastic cup will be worn down by the metal head over time, eventually causing joint failure. Scientists have now developed an all-metal joint, involving a steel cap that fits on the femur and a steel cup that will not wear away.

SPORTS
Almost all sports involve using the legs to a certain degree. Some, such as skiing (left), jumping or running, subject the legs to incredible forces as the feet pound into the ground. Damage to the more vulnerable parts of the limbs, such as the knees and ankles, can occur. You may see many athletes wearing strapping or padding to protect sore areas from any further damage.

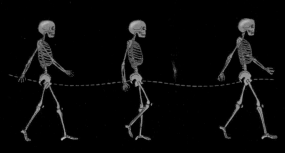

WALKING
Moving one step at a time is actually a controlled way of falling. Each step depends on you losing your balance so that you fall forward. However, before you topple over, you stick out your front leg and, by pushing off with your rear leg, move a step forward. As a result, your body moves up and down as you stride with each leg in turn (above).

18

THE FEMUR

The strongest, heaviest and longest bone in your body, the femur, is positioned so that it slopes in from the hip to the knee (right). This ensures that the bone lies as far under the body's centre of gravity as possible, allowing the femur to support much of the body's weight. The bone is usually one quarter of a person's height and it is strong enough to withstand very intense forces.

FEMUR

PELVIS

Femur

Knee

Fibula

Tibia

— Patella

LOWER LEG

Below the knee, the lower leg is made up of two bones, the fibula and the tibia. The larger tibia supports much of the body's weight, transferring it down from the femur and into the foot. The thin fibula supports little weight, but is essential in controlling the ankle joint at the bottom of the leg.

PATELLA

The knee joint is covered by the largest of the sesamoid bones (see page 7), the patella, or kneecap. Found within the tendon, this bone protects the knee, and increases the muscle power by acting as a pivot around which the muscle can pull the leg.

19

HEEL AND ANKLE

Your heel bone, or calcaneus, sticks out a little from the back of the foot. This provides the muscles at the back of the lower leg with a lever on which they can pull the foot, allowing you to point your toes. The top most ankle bone, or talus, sits against the fibula and tibia and forms the ankle joint.

FIBULA TIBIA

Phalanges

ARCHES OF THE FOOT

Your foot is arched to help absorb the shocks of everyday activity and to help the foot transmit energy from one step to another. Without the arch, your feet would not be able to move about properly or cushion the enormous pressure that every step generates.

Tarsals

Metatarsals

BONES OF THE FOOT

The foot is made up of seven tarsals, or ankle bones, five metatarsals and fourteen phalanges, or toe bones (above). Although it has a small range of movement compared with the hand, its bones act as a vital lever, rotating around the ankle. Without the foot, the body would not be able to walk.

Heal bone

Ankle bone

Bone

Cartilage

Blood supply

Marrow cavity

CARTILAGE

YOUR SKELETON is mostly formed from bone, but it does have parts made from cartilage. There are several types of cartilage – hyaline cartilage, fibro-cartilage and elastic cartilage. They are strong and tough, but less hard and rigid than bone, so they can be bent or squashed slightly and can absorb more pressure without cracking.

At a microscopic level, cartilage has many similarities to bone. It has cells which build and maintain it, called chondrocytes, along with tough fibres of the protein collagen. These are embedded in ground substance, a mixture of various fibres and minerals. However, unlike bone, cartilage has no blood vessels or nerves inside it. Instead, cartilage obtains its nutrients and gets rid of its wastes by diffusion, or seepage, via nearby tissues.

OSSIFICATION

This is the process of replacing cartilage with bone. In a baby, the shapes of most bones are formed in cartilage. Then chondrocyte cells start processes that eat away the cartilage. The chondrocytes die and bone cells begin to lay down minerals and create bony tissue at once. Gradually, the bone re-shapes itself to include blood vessels, nerves and marrow (above).

20

Trachea

Vertebrae

Knee

FIBRO-CARTILAGE

This type of cartilage is packed with more fibres of the protein collagen than other cartilage types (left). This makes fibro-cartilage extremely hard-wearing. Pieces of it form shock-absorbing "washers" in joints where they can absorb high levels of pressure. Fibro-cartilage can be found in joints, such as those between the vertebrae of the spine and between the two pubic bones at the front of the pelvis.

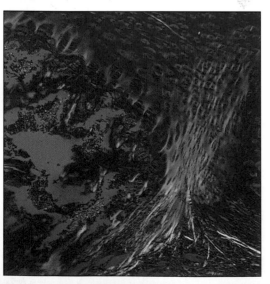

CARTILAGE IN JOINTS

Hyaline cartilage (right) covers many bones at the point where they press on and move past each other inside joints. For example, it covers the ends of the humerus (upper arm bone), radius and ulna (lower arm bones) where they form the elbow joint (left). This prevents wear on the bones and reduces friction, or rubbing, in the joint. In these sites, hyaline cartilage is also called articular cartilage.

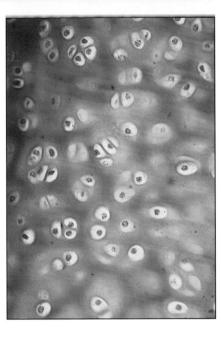

HYALINE CARTILAGE

This type of cartilage is shiny and pearly white, with a large proportion of ground substance (left) and is the most common type of cartilage in the body. It supports several parts of the body, such as the trachea and bronchi (breathing airways) where it forms rings around the tubes and the tip of the nose. It also covers bones inside joints, and forms the majority of an unborn baby's skeleton (see page 24).

ELASTIC CARTILAGE

In addition to collagen fibres and ground substance, this type of cartilage also contains lots of elastic fibres. These make it more flexible than other types of cartilage, though slightly softer. It forms parts that are not subjected to great wear, such as the outer ear (right).

NOSE

The shape of the nose is formed from about a dozen curved plates of hyaline cartilage. A central plate of cartilage splits your nose into two nostrils.

EAR

The outer ear, or ear flap, contains a framework of thin elastic cartilage. This gives the main ear its swirled shape. It is easily bent, but can spring back into place.

21

Adam's apple

ADAM'S APPLE

This protuberance in the neck is formed by the thyroid cartilage. This is the largest of the nine curved pieces of elastic cartilage which make up the voice box, called the larynx.

BETWEEN THE BONES

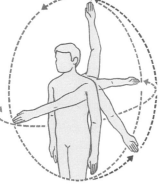

BONES ARE LINKED to each other at joints, of which there are three basic kinds – fibrous, cartilaginous and synovial. In a fibrous joint, the bones are joined tightly by tough fibres, which usually give little or no movement. In a cartilaginous joint, the bones are linked by a lump, strip or block of cartilage. This is slightly flexible in most cases, allowing a small amount of movement.

In synovial joints (the joints shown on page 23 are all synovial joints), the ends of the bones are covered with smooth, wear-resistant cartilage, and the joint contains a lubricant called synovial fluid. Together, these allow synovial joints a much greater range of movement, as with the shoulder (top left).

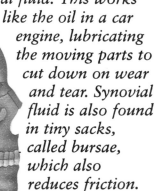

Tendon

FEMUR

Bursae

Fatty pad

Patella

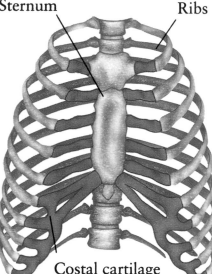

Sternum

Ribs

Costal cartilage

CARTILAGINOUS JOINTS
The junction between a rib and the sternum (breastbone) is known as a cartilaginous joint (left). The bones are joined by bridges of costal cartilage.

These joints include the discs between adjacent vertebrae (see page 12) as well as the joint between the two pubic bones at the front of the pelvis.

SYNOVIAL JOINTS
The knee is one of the body's more complicated joints (above). The bones are held close together by tough straps, called ligaments. These ensure that the joint remains intact even when put under excessive pressure.

The inside of the joint continuously produces tiny amounts of a fluid called synovial fluid. This works like the oil in a car engine, lubricating the moving parts to cut down on wear and tear. Synovial fluid is also found in tiny sacks, called bursae, which also reduces friction.

FIBROUS JOINTS
Examples of these joints are found between the skull bones (right). Fibres grow into the bones and pull them together so that there is no gap between them. These tight joints are called sutures. In adulthood, each suture forms a wiggly line on the skull, and most of the skull becomes one single bone.

Suture joints

PIVOT

A rod of one bone fits into a ring of another (below), allowing it to swivel, as with the bones in the neck.

I n a synovial joint, the strong ligaments holding the bones normally stop them moving too far apart. But excessive force in an unnatural direction can twist the bones and make their ends come apart inside the joint. This is called a dislocation. In this case (below), a dislocation of the knee has resulted in the knee cap (patella) being forced above the joint so that it now rests on the thigh bone (femur).

BALL AND SOCKET

The ball-shaped head of a long bone fits into the cup-shaped socket of another, allowing movement in any direction (above), as with the shoulder.

HINGE

The curved surface of one bone wraps around and fits over the similar curved surface of its neighbour. This allows movement in only one way, as with the elbow (below).

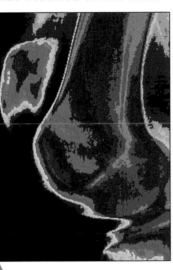

SADDLE

Bone ends that each have saddle-shaped surfaces allow movement in two planes at right angles, such as the joint at the base of the thumb (below).

23

CONDYLOID

This is like a ball and socket joint, but the head of the bone is flatter (below), allowing less movement, as with the knuckle joints.

GLIDING

Two flat bones butt against each other (below). This permits small gliding movements in almost any direction, as with the bones in the wrist and foot.

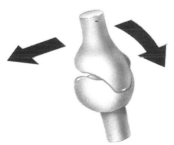

Tibia

Fibula

Ankle bones

LIGAMENTS

In complex joints between many bones, such as in the ankle (left), there is a network of ligaments criss-crossing the area and holding the bones together. Ligaments have a rich nerve supply, so they are sensitive to damage. The pain of a "sprained ankle" may be due to tearing the ligaments on the outside of the foot and ankle.

The GROWING SKELETON

THE HUMAN BODY grows from a thumb-sized foetus at roughly three months after conception to full adult size by about the age of twenty. This is achieved mainly through the growth of the body's skeleton. During these first twenty years of incredible growth, the skeleton continuously rebuilds itself, laying down new minerals, fibres and ground substance to increase the size of its bones.

By the time you've grown into an adult, your total height will only be about 2.5 cm (1 in) greater than the height of your skeleton.

Bone re-absorbed

Bone deposited

HOW BONES LENGTHEN
As you grow into an adult, your long bones, such as those found in your arms and legs, will lengthen steadily. This lengthening will happen in "growth zones" which lie between the head of the bone and its shaft. Just behind the head, bone tissue is re-absorbed. At the same time new bone tissue is deposited along the shaft and at the head, making the bone longer and thicker (above).

Fontanelles

SOFT SPOTS
At birth, a baby's skull has a number of "soft spots", or fontanelles. These are areas where the bone has not grown completely. They allow the skull bones to overlap as the baby passes down the birth canal and let the child's brain grow during the first few years.

INFANT SKELETON
By the age of about one year, the true bone is rapidly replacing the cartilage model. Like the development of the whole body, this process follows a general "head-first" trend. It happens first in the axial skeleton of the skull, spine and ribs, and then in the appendicular skeleton of the limbs (see page 7).

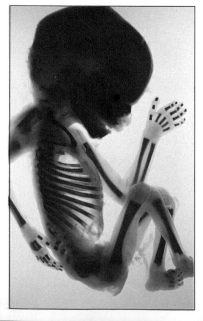

FOETAL SKELETON
The skeleton develops in the foetus first as cartilage instead of bone (left). This foetal skeleton is known as the cartilage model. When the foetus is about eight weeks old, bone tissue starts to replace the cartilage by the process of ossification (see page 20).

BODILY PROPORTIONS

At birth, a baby's head is large compared to the rest of its body. It forms about one-quarter of its total height. Over time, the head's growth slows and gradually the torso catches up. Next, the arms lengthen, and finally the legs grow. In an adult, the head is only about one-eighth of the total height (above). The majority of adult height is decided by the length of the backbone and the leg bones.

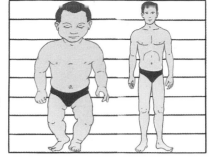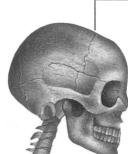

ADULT SKELETON

The growth zones (see page 24) will gradually disappear after you reach the age of 13 to 15 years, when the heads of your long bones fuse with their necks. Other bones will still be developing in the ankles and wrists until you are about 20 years, when you will have reached your full height. However, not all of your bones will be fully mature until you reach about 25 years of age.

TALL AND SMALL

The final size of the adult skeleton, whether it belongs to a tall basketball player (above) or a small jockey (below) is determined largely by the genes inherited from the parents. On average, tall parents tend to have tall children. The size of a skeleton can also be affected by the type of food eaten during growth.

CHILD SKELETON

Growth slows slightly by the age of about six years. It continues at a steady pace until 10 to 12 years in girls, and a year or two later in boys, when the hormonal changes of puberty bring another growth spurt of the skeleton and body. This affects the long bones in particular.

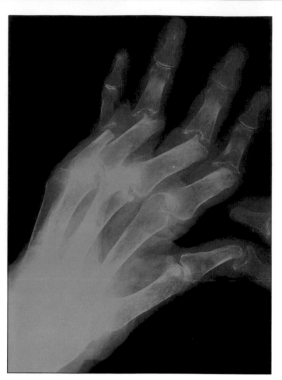

CARTILAGE GROWTH

In some people, the extremities that are supported by cartilage, such as the ears and nose, continue to grow throughout life. At the same time, other body tissues such as skin tend to shrink and thin as part of normal ageing. This combination can make parts such as the nose and ears (especially the lobes) look abnormally large.

OSTEOARTHRITIS

In this type of arthritis, the hyaline cartilage, which covers the ends of the bones in synovial joints, begins to deteriorate. They roughen, flake and crack, perhaps through excessive use or abnormal strains, or from some unknown cause. The affected joints are often the weight-bearing ones such as the knees and hips (left).

RHEUMATOID ARTHRITIS

"Arthritis" means inflammation of a joint, which becomes red, swollen and painful. There are several distinct types. In rheumatoid arthritis (above), the body turns its germ-fighting system against its own tissues, especially the synovial membranes, joint capsules and cartilage. These can become deformed if the disease is bad.

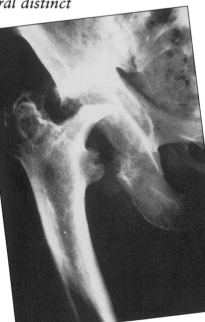

HIPS

These may suffer from various types of arthritis, especially osteoarthritis. Because hip problems cause difficulty in moving, the answer may be a hip replacement (see page 18).

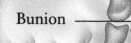

Bunion

BUNIONS

A bunion is an inflamed, tender, painful "lump" on the outside of the big toe in older people. It is usually caused by deformity and swelling of the joint there, and the growth of a fluid-filled bag with thickened skin, or callus, over it. It can be caused by joint weakness or ill-fitting shoes.

KNEES

The knee is vulnerable to twisting. Over time, the cartilage and ligaments may become damaged, especially if the person has played a contact sport such as rugby.

The AGEING SKELETON

THE BODY'S AGEING process is not very noticeable in the skeleton until about the age of 40 to 50. Then the processes of bone and cartilage maintenance (see pages 8-9) begin to fall behind, and they are unable to keep the bones and joints healthy.

Part of this deterioration is bodywide, due to the ageing of the heart and narrowing of the blood vessels, so blood can no longer bring bones enough nutrients or carry away their wastes effectively.

Another aspect is physical wear and tear, since the skeleton is the major body system that experiences the most physical stresses and strains during life. Chemical changes involving hormones and nutrients from food may also be involved.

STOOPED BACK
Another symptom of old age that may affect the skeleton is a stooped appearance and a hunch in the upper back (above). This is caused by a crumbling of vertebrae in the back, which in turn is caused by osteoporosis (see below).

FINGERS
Osteoarthritis affects the knuckle joints and makes the fingers look distorted (see page 26). Rheumatoid arthritis tends to make the knuckles swollen, red and shiny (left).

Spongy bone

Compact bone

HEALTHY BONE

Thinning bone

DISEASED BONE

SHRINKING SKELETON
As bone and cartilage maintenance deteriorates when the body gets older, some tissues tend to shrink slightly, like the skin and many other parts. This is most noticeable in the joints between the vertebrae where the discs of cartilage become thinner. Added up over many bones and joints of the skeleton, this means that the skeleton may shrink quite noticeably in height (right).

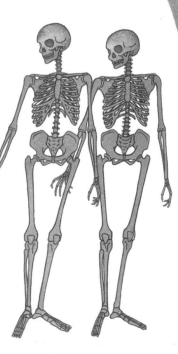

THINNING BONES
Osteoporosis is a disease of the ageing skeleton. The bone tissue becomes wasted, brittle, thin and more spongy (above right). This occurs when a change in the skeleton's maintenance process causes bone tissue to be destroyed more quickly than it can be replaced.

There are many causes, such as general lack of exercise and bodily activity; enforced immobilisation after injury or illness; lack of calcium and other minerals in the diet; and hormonal conditions or changes, especially in older women.

A break in a bone is called a fracture. There are many types of fracture, which vary according to the way the bones are damaged. They can be cracked or snapped right through. Other parts may also be damaged, such as the joints and the surrounding muscles, nerves, blood vessels and skin.

Fractures tend to happen more in children, whose bones are more slender and not as tough as those of an adult. But fractures tend to heal faster in children. A fractured long bone, such as a radius or tibia, is repaired in about four weeks at the age of one year. In a 30-year-old adult this healing may take up to four months.

SIMPLE FRACTURE
The bone is snapped or cracked, but it does not break through the overlying skin, so the risk of infection is lessened. This is also called a closed fracture.

SIMPLE

GREENSTICK

COMMINUTED

COMMINUTED
The bone is crushed, splintered or shattered into many small pieces. It may require a delicate operation to replace as many of the bits as possible, or to transplant a chunk of bone from a less essential part of the skeleton.

GREENSTICK
So called because a supple, growing, green twig curves and then cracks on one side when bent, rather than snapping in two. This is what happens in the flexible bones of children. It is less common in the stiffer bones of adults.

COMPOUND
The broken parts of the bone break through the skin, bringing the risk of infection from germs outside. This is also called an open fracture.

IMPACTED

COMPOUND

IMPACTED
This is usually caused by a force pushing hard along the length of the bone, like falling on an outstretched arm. This causes the shaft to crack and one part of the bone impacts or telescopes into the other. This causes the whole bone to become shorter.

HEALING BONES

O NE OF THE main surprises about bones, which seem so inactive, is that they can rapidly mend themselves after injury, such as being cracked.

This healing process happens naturally and relies on the plentiful blood supply to the bone, but modern medical techniques can also help it. Displaced bones or bone fragments may be replaced in their correct positions (called "setting"), and then supported and stabilised by various methods. This takes stresses off them so they are not strained, and they heal into their natural shapes.

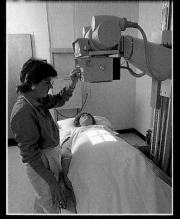

X-RAYS
The most common way of seeing a bone is by an X-ray image. X-rays pass through soft body parts such as muscles. But the rays are stopped by bones, which show up as white on the image.

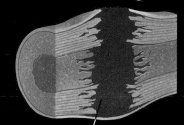

Blood clot

Repaired vessels

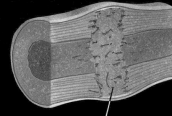

Scar material

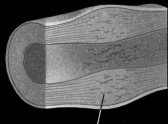

Healed bone

HEALING
A few hours after a fracture takes place, the leaked blood from the damaged blood vessels hardens into a haematoma or blood clot. Blood vessels repair themselves and re-grow into the damaged area. Cells, called fibroblasts, reach the site and multiply, laying down fibrous "scar" material called a callus. Gradually the osteoblast cells take over and replace the callus with spongy bone, which then converts to normal compact bone.

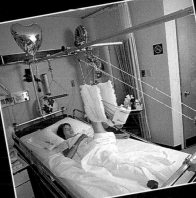

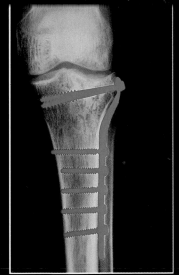

There are many ways to support and stabilise a damaged bone or joint, so that healing happens faster. Internal methods include various plates, strips and pins of metal or plastic (above). These are cemented or screwed to the healthy bone on either side of the site, and they work like built-in splints. They are usually left in place after healing.

Slings, splints or plaster casts hold the damaged body part still and steady from the outside (right).

The muscles around a damaged bone may go into spasm, forcing the broken ends against each other. To relieve this, a patient is put in traction (above), where opposing pulling forces take the strain from the injury.

ALL MAMMALS *have seven cervical vertebrae, or neck bones. That includes you and the long-necked giraffe (below), whose cervical vertebrae have become stretched over millions of years of evolution. This lets the giraffe see for miles over the African plains, as well as letting it reach the juiciest leaves at the tops of trees.*

KNOW YOUR BODY!

WHEN YOU *are very young, you have about 300 bones in your body. As you grow older, some of these bones fuse together, so that by the time you are grown up (right) you will only have 206.*

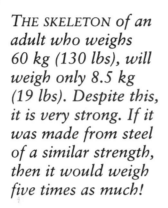

7 Neck Bones

THE SKELETON *of an adult who weighs 60 kg (130 lbs), will weigh only 8.5 kg (19 lbs). Despite this, it is very strong. If it was made from steel of a similar strength, then it would weigh five times as much!*

Calcium

Phosphate

Magnesium

BONES ARE *important for storing minerals in your body (see page 5). Your skeleton holds 99 percent of your body's calcium, 86 percent of your body's phosphate and 54 percent of its magnesium (above left). They are stored as salts and they help to keep the bones rigid. Without them the skeleton would be floppy.*

THE TALLEST *man ever was Robert Wadlow from America (right). When he was born in 1918 he weighed a relatively normal 3.8 kg (8 lbs). However, by the age of eight he had already grown to 183 cm (6 ft) in height, and weighed nearly 77 kg (170 lbs).*

When he died in 1940, aged 22 years, he was 2.7 m (8 ft 11 in) tall. At his heaviest, he weighed 222.7 kg (490 lbs).

The tallest woman was Zeng Jinlian from China, who grew to 2.4 m (8 ft 1 in).

SKELETONS FOUND *in laboratories are white because their bones have been lightened in colour. The bones of a living skeleton can vary in colour from beige or light brown to pink.*

GLOSSARY

Appendicular skeleton – The part of the skeleton made up of the shoulders, arms, hips and legs.

Arthritis – A disease which attacks joints causing them to swell.

Axial skeleton – The part of the skeleton made up of the skull, backbone and the ribcage.

Bone – Hard tissue made up of fibres of collagen, mineral crystals and ground substance. It is also called osseous tissue.

Bone marrow – The soft tissue that fills the cavity in the shafts of bones.

Cartilage – Also called "gristle", this tissue provides support and helps with movement in joints.

Centre of gravity – The point through which the weight of the body is said to act. In you this sits in the hips.

Collagen – A protein that can form long fibres found in bone and cartilage.

Compact bone – A hard tissue, made up of cylinders of bone called Haversian systems.

Fracture – A broken bone, which can be slightly cracked or snapped in two.

Ground substance – A mixture of substances found around the bone and cartilage cells, it helps with the transport of nutrients and waste.

Growth zone – The region of a bone where old bone tissue is resorbed and new tissue is laid down. In long bones it is found between the head and the neck of the bone.

Haversian system – A tube-like structure. Thousands of these make up compact bone tissue.

Joint – Any point where two or more bones meet. There are several types, including synovial, cartilaginous and fibrous.

Lamellae – The tiny layers of bone tissue that surround the Haversian canal. These form part of the Haversian systems found in compact bone.

Ligament – A thick, fibrous cord that joins one bone to another, allowing movement of the joint.

Ossification – The process by which cartilage is broken down and replaced with bone tissue.

Osteocyte – A bone cell capable of releasing calcium from bone tissue and into blood. It is found in mature bone tissue.

Periosteum – The fibrous covering found on the outside of bones, which contains the bone-forming cells and blood vessels.

Sinus – An air space found in the skull. It aids in sound production and makes the skull lighter.

Skeleton – A body's supporting structure, which can be found inside, as with humans, or outside, as with insects.

Spongy bone – Also called cancellous bone, this occurs when bone tissue forms an open, interlaced pattern, with fingers of bone surrounded by spaces filled with marrow.

Synovial fluid – Found within the capsule of a synovial joint, this fluid lubricates the joint, protecting it from wear.

Tendon – A strong cord, made from fibres of collagen, which attaches a muscle to a bone.

X-ray – A form of radiation that can produce an image of hard internal parts, such as bone, on a special photographic plate.

INDEX

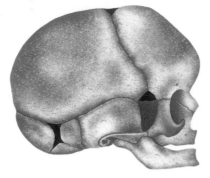

Adam's apple 11, 21
ageing 26-27
animals 4-5
appendicular skeleton 6-7, 24, 31
arm bones 16
arthritis 26, 31
axial skeleton 6-7, 24, 31
backbone 4, 6, 12
blood cells 5, 8
blood vessels 8, 9, 20, 27
bone marrow 8, 9, 20, 31
bone, types of 6-7, 9
brain 5, 10
breathing 14, 15
cartilage 5, 12, 14, 15, 20-21, 24, 26, 27
clavicles 15
coccyx 12, 13
cochlea 11
collagen 20, 31
compact bone 8, 9, 29, 31
diaphragm 15
ear bones 10, 11
exoskeleton 14

fontanelles 24
foot bones 19
fractures 28-29, 31
grip 17
ground substance 20, 21, 24, 31
growth 24-25
Haversian canal 9, 31
hand bones 17

hip bones 18
horse 4
hyoid bone 11
jaw bones 10, 11
jellyfish 4
joints 10, 22-23, 26, 31
lamellae 9, 31
larynx 21
leg bones 18-19
ligaments 11, 22, 23, 26, 31

leukemia 8
lobster 4
mammals 4, 5
minerals 5, 24, 30
nerves 12, 13, 20
ossification 20, 24, 31
osteocytes 9, 31
osteoporosis 27
patellas 19, 22, 23
pelvis 12, 13
periosteum 8, 31
rays 5
ribcage 7, 14-15
sacrum 12, 13
sea lion 16
shoulder blades 6, 16
sinuses 11, 31
skull 5, 7, 10-11, 22, 24
slipped disc 13
spinal cord 12
spine 7, 12-13, 24
spongy bone 8, 9, 29, 31
sternum 6, 14, 15, 22
tendon 7, 22, 31
tissue 8, 20, 26
vertebrae 6, 12, 13, 14, 15, 30
vertebrate 4
vocal cords 11
walking 5, 18
X-rays 3, 5, 29, 31

Photo credits:
Abbreviations: t-top, m-middle, b-bottom, r-right, l-left

Cover m, 5b, 10-11, 13, 14-15, 17tr, 20-21, 21bl & br, 26-27 & 29b – Roger Vlitos. Cover mr, 3b, 7, 8 both, 9 both, 11, 17m, 18m, 20, 21t, 23, 24, 26 both, 29tl & tr & m – Science Photo Library. 3t, 17tl, 18b, 25m & 27 – Frank Spooner Pictures. 4 – Bruce coleman Collection. 12, 14 & 16 – Eye Ubiquitous. 25b – Rex Features. 30t – Spectrum Colour Library. 20b – Hulton Getty Collection.